A TRUE BOOK™

Women's History in the U.S.

WOMEN
in
World War II

Susan Taylor

Children's Press®
An Imprint of Scholastic Inc.

Content Consultant
Holly Hynson, MA
Department of History
University of Maryland, College Park

Thank you to Elise McMullen-Ciotti for her insights into Indigenous Peoples' history and culture.

A CIP catalog record of this book is available from the Library of Congress.
ISBN 978-0-531-13081-0 (library binding) 978-0-531-13340-8 (paperback)

Scholastic Inc., 557 Broadway, New York, NY 10012

1 2 3 4 5 6 7 8 9 10 R 30 29 28 27 26 25 24 23 22 21

Book produced by 22 MEDIAWORKS, INC.
Book design by Amelia Leon / Fabia Wargin Design

Front Cover: During World War II, women stepped into jobs traditionally held by men.
Back Cover: Women who served in the Navy joined the WAVES (Women Accepted for Volunteer Emergency Service).

Find the Truth

Everything you are about to read is true *except* for one of the sentences on this page.

Which one is **TRUE**?

T or F   During World War II, skilled men and women in the workforce earned the same wages.

T or F   More nurses served in World War II than in any other war in American history.

Find the answers in this book.

Contents

Harriet Ida Pickens and Frances Elizabeth Wills

1 Women Join Forces

2 Support for the Troops

The **BIG** Truth

Women in the Air Force were known as WASPs.

Denied Equal Rights

Photojournalist Lee Miller with soldiers at the front.

Rosie the Riveter

INTRODUCTION
The World at War

World War II involved all the world's major countries. **From 1939 to 1945,** Germany, Japan, and Italy, known as **the Axis** powers, fought Britain, the United States, and the Soviet Union, among others, known as the **Allied** powers.

Adolf Hitler, the leader of Germany, wanted to make his country more powerful by expanding its territory. As the German army

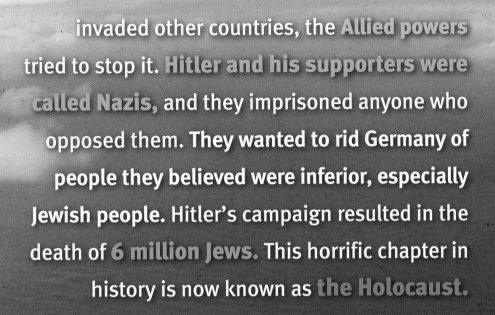

invaded other countries, the Allied powers tried to stop it. Hitler and his supporters were called Nazis, and they imprisoned anyone who opposed them. They wanted to rid Germany of people they believed were inferior, especially Jewish people. Hitler's campaign resulted in the death of 6 million Jews. This horrific chapter in history is now known as the Holocaust.

Bombers were a common type of aircraft used during World War II. They could carry heavy loads and fly long distances.

The country of Japan also wanted to expand its empire and control the Pacific Ocean. In 1941, Japan attacked the United States at the port of Pearl Harbor in Hawaii, killing over 2,000 American servicemen and **civilians**. In response, the U.S. declared war on Japan and joined the Allies to defeat the Axis powers.

The war was long, deadly, and affected nearly every country around the world.

In May 1945, Germany surrendered after losing several big battles in Europe. The war finally ended in August after Japan surrendered.

Everyone in the United States contributed in some way to the war effort. **Women especially stepped into roles that they had not traditionally held.**

They built airplanes, drove ambulances, and took over jobs that men left behind when they went to war. **These jobs created new opportunities and new expectations for women around the country.**

More than 2,000 Americans lost their lives during the attack on Pearl Harbor. Female nurses cared for many of the injured soldiers.

9

About 350,000 U.S. women joined the military during World War II.

Members of the Women's Army Corps traveled overseas to help the Allies win the war. Traveling by ship from America to France took about a week.

Women Join Forces

Between 1941 and 1944, hundreds of thousands of women voluntarily joined the war effort. Although women were not allowed in **combat**, they were able to join the **military** in other ways. With men on the front lines, women were needed to fill important jobs in each of the five main branches of the military: the U.S. Army, Air Force, Navy, Marines, and Coast Guard.

Women in the Army

The first women's division in the military was the Women's Army Auxiliary Corps (WAAC), formed in 1942. Women in the WAAC worked as telephone operators, mail sorters, and mechanics. This division became so popular that the Army made the group an official branch. The name was changed to the Women's Army Corps (WAC). Thanks to this change, the women received better pay and benefits.

Oveta Culp Hobby was the first director of the Women's Army Corps.

The uniforms for women in the Army included a skirt and a fitted jacket.

Major Charity Adams Earley led the first group of African Americans in the WAC to serve overseas.

One of the first women to join the WAC was Charity Adams Earley. She was one of nearly 6,500 African American women who joined the WAC between 1942 and 1945. Because of the color of their skin, these women were **segregated** from white women in the military. Earley led an all-Black unit that traveled overseas and delivered backlogged mail for 7 million soldiers who were fighting. For her efforts, Earley was promoted to lieutenant colonel, the highest possible position for women in the WAC.

Women in the Air Force

During World War II, pilots used airplanes and helicopters to fight against the enemy. After the Women Airforce Service Pilots (WASPs) formed in 1943, women trained as pilots and mechanics, and air traffic controllers. However, women were not allowed to fly in combat. They worked as test pilots and flew planes from one base to another. Thirty-eight of these women died in service.

Four female pilots finish a training exercise flying a B-17. WASPs flew almost every type of aircraft.

Over 25,000 women applied to join the Air Force, but only 1,879 were accepted.

Earning Respect

Not everyone liked the idea of women serving in the military. In the Air Force, women were needed to fill in for the shortage of pilots, but they were not always respected by men they worked with. Some men thought that women didn't have the strength or courage to fly in bad weather or pack heavy parachutes. The commanding general of the Air Force during the war, Henry Arnold, said at first that he didn't think women could live up to the challenge. But more than 1,100 female pilots in the program proved him wrong. In a speech near the end of the war, he admitted, "Now in 1944, it is on the record that women can fly as well as men."

WASPs flew every type of mission male Air Force pilots flew during World War II, except combat.

Women in the Navy

WAVES write down data during an inspection and test firing exercise during World War II.

Battleships, submarines, and other Navy craft carried soldiers all around the world during the war. In 1942, Congress formed the Women Accepted for Volunteer Emergency Service (WAVES). The Navy relied on women to fill jobs aboard these vessels. The new unit freed even more men to fight overseas. Women in the WAVES also helped at home in the United States, in **clerical** jobs and working in hospitals. More than 85,000 women joined the Navy, but women of color were not common. Only 72 African American women served in the WAVES.

When the United States entered the war, Asian American Susan Ahn Cuddy wanted to serve her country. Cuddy applied to Naval Officer School but was rejected. Although her family background was Korean, not Japanese, many people distrusted anyone who seemed to be of Asian descent. But she didn't give up. She applied again, and this time was accepted. Cuddy became the first Asian American woman to join the WAVES and spent the rest of the war teaching new male recruits how to shoot down enemy airplanes.

After the war, Susan Ahn Cuddy continued working for the Navy, breaking coded messages for more than a decade.

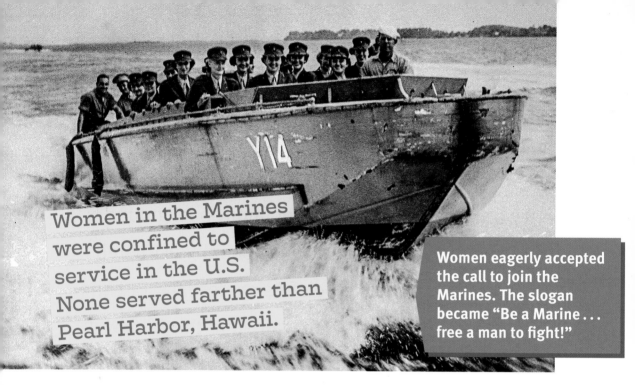

Women in the Marines were confined to service in the U.S. None served farther than Pearl Harbor, Hawaii.

Women eagerly accepted the call to join the Marines. The slogan became "Be a Marine ... free a man to fight!"

Women in the Marines

Marines are usually the first wave of military personnel deployed in any conflict. They specialize in ship-to-land operations. In 1943, the Marines opened recruitment to women. Over 20,000 women were selected for noncombat roles. They worked as welders, mechanics, and radio operators, among other positions.

Women in the Coast Guard

The Coast Guard branch for women was called SPARS. The SPARS were the first women to attend a military academy. More than 700 women trained at the Coast Guard Academy to do clerical work and to become radio operators, cooks, and drivers. SPARS also operated a new technology called LORAN that could identify the exact location of enemy ships along the coast.

SPARS

APPLY NEAREST COAST GUARD OFFICE

SPARS posters helped recruit women to the Coast Guard program. Recruiting was sometimes a challenge because SPARS was not as popular as other units.

U.S. Army nurses practice using gas masks. Nurses trained for four weeks, learning important military skills.

There were only 1,000 nurses in the Army at the start of World War II. By the end of the war, over 59,000 had served.

CHAPTER

Support for the Troops

World War II required more nurses than any other war. Nurses were needed in the military and in organizations like the American Red Cross. These women risked their lives by working close to the front lines and on trains, ships, and planes. They bandaged wounds, administered anesthetics, and supported soldiers' mental health. The work was difficult and often dangerous.

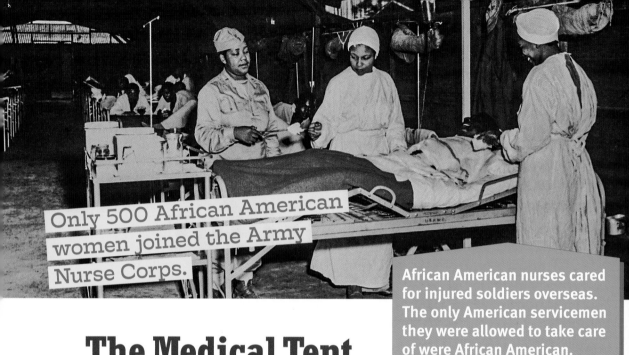

Only 500 African American women joined the Army Nurse Corps.

African American nurses cared for injured soldiers overseas. The only American servicemen they were allowed to take care of were African American.

The Medical Tent

The Army Nurse Corps was an important branch of the military since its founding in 1901. In World War II, nurses often worked in overcrowded field hospitals where there were more injured soldiers than beds. Some nurses worked 12 hour days, with no time off.

African American nurses were given the least desirable nursing tasks, including caring for enemy German prisoners. These women lived in segregated quarters.

While most nurses were women, most doctors were men. In 1943, President Roosevelt signed a bill allowing female doctors to **enlist**. Soon after, Yale Medical School graduate Margaret Craighill joined the Army Medical Corps. She became the first female doctor to serve in the Army. Craighill visited war zones and examined and reported on the condition of Army nurses and WAC servicewomen. She enthusiastically supported the work of women in the military.

An Army nurse (right) and doctor tend to a patient at an overcrowded makeshift hospital housed in a church in the Philippines in 1944.

Aid and Entertainment

The American Red Cross also supplied support for troops during the war. Millions of volunteers, mostly women, recruited people to donate blood. They attended to injured soldiers by writing letters for them as well as lifting their spirits.

Women in other nonmilitary organizations provided recreation and entertainment, boosting **morale** for soldiers. The United Service Organizations (USO) was one of these groups.

A woman performs at a concert at a USO camp in France in 1944. Volunteers traveled to the front lines to put on shows and support the troops.

Eleanor Roosevelt

First lady Eleanor Roosevelt, wife of President Franklin D. Roosevelt, encouraged women to help the war effort. Through her radio programs and newspaper articles, she urged women to volunteer for the Red Cross or find meaningful work outside the home. She also traveled overseas to visit troops. She toured places that had been bombed and met with women's military organizations. One admiral said of her visit, "She alone accomplished more good than any other person, or groups of civilians, who had passed through my area."

The first lady presents a book to a volunteer nurse's aide at a Red Cross event. The Red Cross urged Americans to donate books to servicemen.

The **BIG** Truth

Denied Equal Rights

Some people thought it wasn't appropriate for women to serve in the military or work as mechanics, engineers, or pilots. As a result, many women faced **discrimination** during the war. Here are a few examples of what this discrimination looked like:

Unequal Recognition

During the war and its aftermath, women were rarely recognized for their efforts. It was more than 50 years before the WASPs received the Congressional Gold Medal, the highest award Congress can give to civilians.

Former WASP pilot Betty Wall Strohfus holds up a picture of herself during World War II.

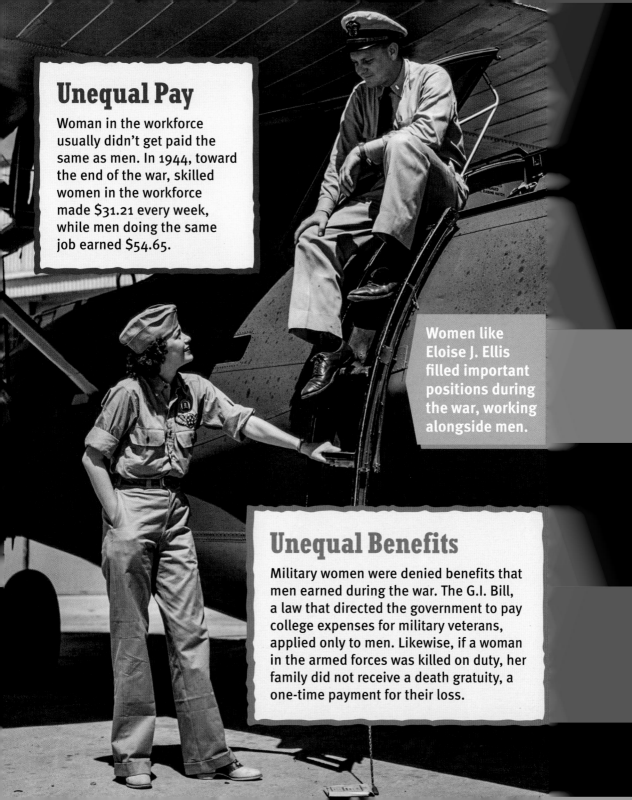

Unequal Pay

Woman in the workforce usually didn't get paid the same as men. In 1944, toward the end of the war, skilled women in the workforce made $31.21 every week, while men doing the same job earned $54.65.

Women like Eloise J. Ellis filled important positions during the war, working alongside men.

Unequal Benefits

Military women were denied benefits that men earned during the war. The G.I. Bill, a law that directed the government to pay college expenses for military veterans, applied only to men. Likewise, if a woman in the armed forces was killed on duty, her family did not receive a death gratuity, a one-time payment for their loss.

Agent Claire Phillips worked as a spy throughout the war, smuggling important documents and supplies to soldiers overseas. Here she is honored on her return to America.

⭐ **3**

Women as Spies

During World War II, spies worked undercover to gather information about the enemy. Women were **conscripted** as undercover agents and radio transmitters to gather sensitive information and send it to leaders at home. The work was top secret and often dangerous. One reason for their success was that German soldiers did not see women around them as a threat.

Secret Messages

Code breakers unscrambled coded messages from the enemy. During the war, one-third of them were women.

Women also worked as radio operators, passing information to leaders in Washington, D.C. They relied on soldiers from the Navajo Nation to create messages in the Navajo language that enemies could not understand. Women like Winnie Breegle learned the Navajo language and translated the coded messages for military leaders.

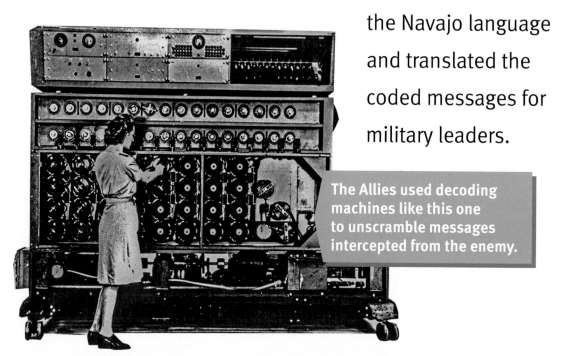

The Allies used decoding machines like this one to unscramble messages intercepted from the enemy.

The Limping Lady

Virginia Hall was an American spy who worked in France, helping prisoners of war escape and gathering information about the enemy. She mapped **drop zones**, trained resistance forces, and found secure locations

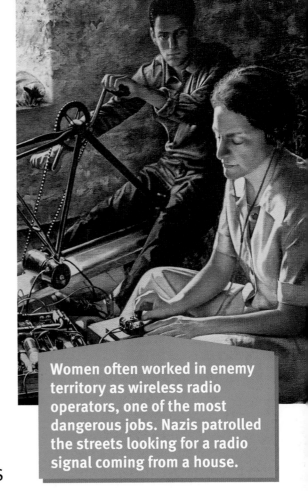

Women often worked in enemy territory as wireless radio operators, one of the most dangerous jobs. Nazis patrolled the streets looking for a radio signal coming from a house.

where she could send information back to the United States Intelligence Agency. Germans knew her as "the limping lady," because she had an artificial leg due to an accident. Hall was the only civilian woman to be awarded the Distinguished Service Cross, the nation's second highest military award, after the war.

The Women's Land Army planted seeds and harvested crops to provide food for the country.

By 1944, women held one-third of all manufacturing jobs in the U.S.

From the Home Front

The war did not only radically change the lives of those that had to travel overseas. Millions of people who stayed in the U.S., especially women, made sacrifices to support the war. They grew their own vegetables in backyard "victory gardens" so farm crops could be sent to feed the troops. They collected metal waste so it could be recycled into war products. Many women took new jobs in munitions and aircraft factories.

The iconic image of Rosie the Riveter represented thousands of women who worked in manufacturing during World War II. One such woman was Anne Isgar, who built airplanes during the war.

Rosie the Riveter

The United States recruited women to help the war through propaganda posters. Some posters encouraged women to join the military while others asked them to join the workforce. One of the most famous posters featured "Rosie the Riveter." The poster pictures a woman who worked as a riveter, a person who built and fixed airplane wings.

All-American Girls

With men off to war, there were no professional sports teams to entertain the nation. So a women's professional baseball league was formed. It played from 1943 until 1954. Nearly 1 million fans attended games. The All-American Girls Professional Baseball League gave women athletes a chance to play professionally, traveling the country and earning good wages.

More than 600 women played in the All-American Girls Professional Baseball League.

Volunteers at Home

Besides the American Red Cross, many associations of volunteers were formed. One of them was the American Women's Voluntary Services. It grouped women who could drive trucks and ambulances, sell war bonds (special funds the government used to pay for the war), take aerial photographs, and work in cafeterias on the home front. The organization included many African American women and other women of color. Nearly 325,000 women had volunteered by the end of the war.

D-Day Dames

As the war was ending, a key battle between the Allies and Germany was fought on the beaches of northern France. This is known as "D-Day." Several women reporters and war correspondents traveled to France to report on the conflict. However, these women weren't allowed on the front lines. One of those journalists was Martha Gellhorn, who hid in a bathroom of a hospital ship. Once the battle was over, she waded ashore to interview the victorious Allied soldiers.

Photographer Lee Miller joins American soldiers to report on the war for readers of *Vogue* magazine.

By 1945, nearly one out of every four women worked outside the home.

Uniformed women celebrate the end of World War II on August 14, 1945.

CHAPTER

5

After the War

By 1945, the United States and its allies had triumphed over the Axis powers. During the war, millions of women had entered the workforce, gained new skills, and served in leadership positions at home and abroad. They had stepped outside their traditional roles and pushed new boundaries. After the war, some of these women found they had new opportunities.

But not all women had the same experience...

Progress Restricted

Millions of men were coming home from the war, and most women found themselves replaced by returning soldiers. In the military, all the female units were eliminated, except for the WAC. Women were limited to 2 percent of the workforce and could not be promoted above the rank of officer. It would be decades before changes regarding women in the military were made.

Timeline: Women Throughout World War II

May 14
Congress creates the WAAC, which allows women to serve in the Army.

November 23
SPARS is established to allow women in the Coast Guard.

1941

1942

December 7
Japan attacks Pearl Harbor. Dozens of nurses stationed there care for injured soldiers.

July 30
WAVES is established to allow women in the Navy. Months later, Mildred McAfee becomes lieutenant commander and the first female officer in U.S. Navy history.

A Movement Started

Despite the fact that many women had to return to old roles after the war, World War II changed some things for women. Jobs as pilots, doctors, or engineers, which had previously been unavailable, seemed within reach now. These changes were the early sparks for the women's movement that was so important during the second half of the 20th century. 🇺🇸

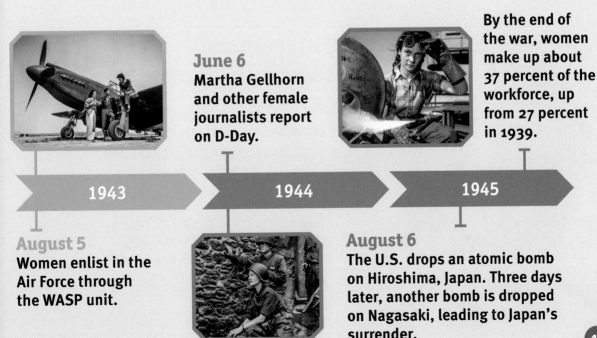

June 6
Martha Gellhorn and other female journalists report on D-Day.

By the end of the war, women make up about 37 percent of the workforce, up from 27 percent in 1939.

1943   **1944**   **1945**

August 5
Women enlist in the Air Force through the WASP unit.

August 6
The U.S. drops an atomic bomb on Hiroshima, Japan. Three days later, another bomb is dropped on Nagasaki, leading to Japan's surrender.

More Women Who Shaped the War

⭐ Captain Dorothy Stratton

(1899–2006) Stratton was the first commanding officer of SPARS. She helped create the name "SPARS." It stood for the motto of the Coast Guard, "Semper Paratus," which means "Always Ready." During her four years as director of the unit, she led over 10,000 women.

⭐ Lieutenant Julia (Nashanany) Reeves

(1919–1998) Lieutenant Reeves was an Indigenous woman from the Forest County Potawatomie in Wisconsin. She joined the Army Nurse Corps in 1942 and traveled to the Pacific in a hospital ship. Later, she was stationed at a hospital in England where she served during D-Day in 1944. During the Korean War, Reeves served at a field hospital.

⭐ Eva Mozes Kor (1934–2019)

After surviving the Holocaust, Eva Mozes Kor moved to the United States to start a new life. She shared her story and talked about the power of forgiveness. Later in life, she revisited Auschwitz, the concentration camp where she had been imprisoned during the war. She went on to create a Holocaust museum to educate people about the war.

⭐ Harriet Ida Pickens (1882–1980) and Frances Elizabeth Wills (1899–1983) ⭐

Harriet Ida Pickens (left) and Frances Elizabeth Wills (right) were the first Black women to receive commissions from the U.S. Navy. In 1944, the two women enlisted in the WAVES, becoming the first of 72 Black women to join the unit. They were stationed at the WAVES training center at Hunter College in New York City.

True Statistics

Number of nurses who served during World War II, the most in history: 60,000

Number of women who served in the WAC: 150,000

Number of Indigenous women who served in World War II: 800

Number of women in the labor force at the height of the war: 19,170,000

Number of U.S. women in all branches of the armed forces during World War II: 350,000

Percentage of women employed in 1939: 27 percent

Percentage of women employed in 1944: 37 percent

Percentage of women who wanted to keep their jobs after the war, according to polls: 61 to 85 percent

Percentage of active duty military members today who are women: 16 percent

Did you find the truth?

F During World War II, skilled men and women in the workforce earned the same wages.

T More nurses served in World War II than in any other war in American history.

Resources

Further Reading

Dell, Pamela. *The Soviet Night Witches: Brave Women Bomber Pilots of World War II*. North Mankato, MN: Capstone Press, 2018.

Funke, Teresa R. *Dancing in Combat Boots: And Other Stories of American Women in World War II*. Fort Collins, CO: Victory House Press, 2007.

Langley, Andrew. *Stories of Women in World War II: We Can Do It!* Chicago: Heinemann Raintree, 2015.

Mundy, Liza. *Code Girls: The True Story of the American Women Who Secretly Broke Codes in World War II*. New York: Little, Brown, 2018.

Simons, Lisa M. Bolt. *The U.S. WASP: Trailblazing Women Pilots of World War II*. North Mankato, MN: Capstone Press, 2018.

Other Books in the Series

 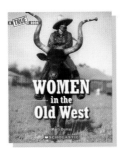 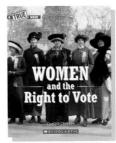 

Glossary

civilians (suh-VIL-yuhnz) people who are not members of the armed forces or a police force

clerical (KLER-i-kuhl) of or having to do with office work, especially routine work such as filing

combat (KAHM-bat) fighting between people or armies

conscripted (kon-SKRIP-ted) enlisted in the armed services

discrimination (dis-krim-i-NAY-shun) prejudice or unfair behavior to others based on differences in such things as age, race, or gender

drop zones (drahp zonz) designated areas into which troops or supplies are dropped by parachute or in which skydivers land

enlist (en-LIST) to join one of the armed forces

military (MIL-i-ter-ee) the armed forces of a country, such as the army or navy

morale (muh-RAL) the mood or spirit of a person or group

segregated (SEG-ri-gay-ted) separated from the main group

Index

Page numbers in **bold** indicate illustrations.

About the Author

Susan Taylor has spent a decade writing for both children and adults. Her work has appeared in *Popular Science*, The History Channel publications, *National Geographic*, Benchmark Books, and elsewhere. In addition to writing, Susan is raising two children and works for the YMCA as a program director, organizing activities for kids ages 0 to 99. Using her undergraduate degree in environmental studies, she educates kids and families about the natural world. She lives with her family in Estes Park, Colorado, where she enjoys hiking, skiing, and camping.